TRIBE of WOMEN

TRIBE of WOMEN

A Photojournalist Chronicles the Lives
of Her Sisters around the Globe

TEXT AND PHOTOGRAPHS BY
CONNIE BICKMAN

New World Library
Novato, California

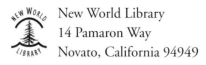

New World Library
14 Pamaron Way
Novato, California 94949

Cover design: Mary Ann Casler
Text design and layout: Mary Ann Casler

Library of Congress Cataloging-in-Publication Data
Bickman, Connie.
Tribe of women : a photojournalist chronicles the lives of her
sisters around the globe / text and photographs by Connie Bickman.
   p. cm.
   ISBN 1-57731-130-2 (alk. paper)
   1. Women—Pictorial works.   I. Title.
HQ1122 .B578 2001
779'.24—dc21   00-013265

First printing, April 2001
ISBN 1-57731-130-2
Printed in Korea on acid-free paper
Distributed to the trade by Publishers Group West

10 9 8 7 6 5 4 3 2 1

To

June and Dolores
my mothers in spirit

To

Cris, Kelli, Nicole,
Jennifer, Cassie, Taylor, Paige, Devin,
and my cat, Ghinsu
my own tribe of women

To

the strength of the Magnolias,
the love and support of good friends,
and the guidance of spirit

To

Mother Earth, who sustains us
with her generous and compassionate
gifts of abundance

To

women everywhere

Namaste

Contents

Author's Preface · Dizzy with the Fragrance of Lilacs

My spiritual journey began subconsciously, long before I ever realized the meaning of the word *spirituality*.

I came from a Lutheran background, changing to Catholic in my late teens. Like many people, I intertwined *religion* and *spirituality* into one bible of truth. Yet I couldn't quite understand many concepts of organized religion, especially when I compared Catholic and Lutheran practices. Why did I have to go to a priest to admit my "sins" now, when for the past seventeen years I had been praying directly to God for forgiveness? Why was I supposed to pray to Mary for assistance when I always went directly to the Source before? Was I supposed to discontinue my direct dialogue with God and go through the "proper" channels? To confuse things even more, my brothers turned Baptist and preached that I was supposed to pray only to Jesus to save my soul from damnation.

I grew up in the country and small Minnesota towns and moved to the big city of Phoenix, Arizona, while still in high school. What a change and an eye-opener for a country farm girl! As the fast pace of city life swallowed me up, I realized that many of my values were still different from those of my peers. My values were simpler. I had close friends but often felt like I just didn't fit in. I was too innocent for the big city life, and I preferred it that way.

I recalled my childhood when I would disappear into my own world of nature on the farm. I made castles in the woods out of leaves and branches and stones and whatever I could find in the forest and pastures. I would play with the fairies, my dolls, my cat, and make-believe friends. I danced with a whirlwind of leaves and floating white wisps of dandelion puffs. I felt like I was one with nature and all her gifts.

I had a secret room in the center of a maze of lilac bushes where I drew pictures and wrote stories that only I would read. I tied ribbons on branches and propped my special treasures into bunches of leaves and made this my inner sanctuary. The smell of lilac perfume made me dizzy. I spent hours by myself, but I was never really alone.

Traveling from childhood through teenage years into adulthood, I often wondered where I should be or what I should be doing with my life. I sensed there was something meaningful waiting for me, something more. Something I was meant to do...

I settled down with a family of my own and as my children grew into beautiful young women I realized that I longed for that world of my own childhood innocence

"When one door of happiness closes, another opens. But often we look so long at the closed door that we do not see the one which has been opened for us."

— Helen Keller

again. The world of simplicity and attunement with nature. I could hear my inner child calling me. I knew I couldn't step back completely; I had wandered too far. But I felt a tug on my soul until finally I answered a resounding, "YES! The child is still in here! Talk to me! Tell me what to do with my life!"

As my three daughters grew I often told them, "You are only limited by yourself." I finally decided I should listen to my own advice and took a long look at my life. I made a list of what I liked and disliked about it and it was clear that I was not living the life of my spirit. I'd limited myself. I'd put my creativity in a glass jar. It could see the outside but could not breathe fresh air or touch blossoming flowers that grew outside the invisible walls. I longed for that dizzy fragrance of lilacs.

That's when I began to live from the inside out.

At forty-something, I began to listen, to honor my inner voice. I realized my soul's purpose was to be a messenger. I relearned to follow my own drumbeat, dance my own dance. I discovered a road of adventure. Cultural richness. Intrigue. Spirituality. My creative soul was free, and I realized my passion. Life would never be the same.

I began to travel the world, and through my journeys I experienced a common thread of unity that wove its way around the earth. Like an enormous human tapestry, it begged to be admired for its fine detail and to be loved for its individuality. I learned to touch the earth, to feel its pulse, to smell the fiber of its roots. To respect the life and cultures of all lands.

My own spiritual center developed out of experiences with Aboriginal elders, Amazon shamans, rain forest bush doctors, nuns, Tibetan rinpoches, Buddhist monks, priests, nomads, visionaries, psychics, and, most significantly, the simple genuine wisdom of other women.

I saw how women in other cultures survive and thrive. I felt the similarities and differences that unite women and grow them strong. I encountered shy smiles and hardy handshakes, long conversations and bold eyes that challenged mine.

I listened to women taught to be submissive to men because of religion or cultural standards. They shared how their spirits were longing, fighting to be free. How they worried for the future of their children, for the safety and security of their own lives.

I learned from women who were in positions of deep respect and power. They spoke their fears and hopes. They also worried for their children. I felt their frustration, their hope, their pain . . . and their strength.

"I have felt the swaying of the elephant's shoulders and you want me to climb on a jackass! Try to be serious!"

— Mirabai
(East Indian poet)

The women I met and photographed taught me to honor and respect the beliefs and disbeliefs, the differences and indifferences of other nations, other women, and of other people. They represent how important it is to honor and respect all sisters and brothers, all neighbors — every gender, color, culture, creed, being, and creature. And to celebrate and care for our earth.

Life depends on it.

I also realized that I didn't have to have a "name" for my spirituality. I was a part of Christianity and Buddhism, Hinduism, Taoism, and Judaism. I found there are many ways to honor the Creator, not just one way. As children of God's light, we are a part of all beliefs, all nature, and all that is. We are God's light.

And as I journeyed I knew that I had returned to the forest. That I was again dancing in the whirlwind with the spirits of my youth. I had worked my way back to the inner maze of my childhood sanctuary and was again dizzy with the fragrance of lilacs.

I invite you to share my journeys through the personal photographs and journal entries in this book. Dance with me into the pages of my travels.

"Now more than ever do I realize that I shall never be content with a sedentary life, and that I shall always be haunted by thoughts of a sun-drenched elsewhere."

— Isabelle Eberhardt

"The future belongs to those who believe in the beauty of their dreams."

— Eleanor Roosevelt

Australia

Peru

Turkey

Namibia

Egypt

Tanzania

Panama

Belize

Nepal

India

Israel

Russia

Ecuador

Yugoslavia

Trinidad

Tobago

United States

Chile

Aboriginal boys at corroboree

Australia, 1989 · Aboriginal Corroboree

Aborigines had gathered in Northern Queensland from all over Australia to participate in an annual corroboree, a celebration of ancestors and culture. I wandered around the ceremonial grounds photographing tribal dances, didgeridoo competitions, fire starting, and boomerang throwing contests. It was a festive atmosphere. People were proud of their heritage and young and old were enjoying this annual reunion of tribes.

As I wandered I noticed a little girl in the shadows, following me, never getting too close, yet near enough to be obvious. Finally I turned, smiled at her and said, "Hello, how are you today?"

Her eyes widened in surprise. She hadn't expected me to speak to her. Maybe she was startled by our ability to communicate in English. She answered in a clear voice, "I'm hot!" A wide, earnest smile spread from ear to ear revealing a row of straight teeth that seemed whiter than they really were against the deep dark brown of her Aboriginal complexion. She came closer and, to my surprise, reached out and touched my hand.

"Are you dancing in the ring today?" I asked.

She shook her head "no" and said, "I like your accent."

I laughed, gently patting her arm. "I like your accent too."

It was interesting that the rough outback appearance of the Aboriginal children hardly seemed to fit the beautiful Australian accent behind their words. Even though there are over seven hundred dialects among the Aboriginal tribes, many of the people also speak English.

"What is your name?" I questioned.

"Lydia," she replied.

I glanced up, hearing giggles from the many children who had gathered around us. Standing politely and watching, they noticed

Aboriginal dancer

Lydia

this new friendship and bravely began to move closer. These brown-bodied, inquisitive children lost their shyness and looked into my camera lens, fondled my crystal necklace, and touched my earrings. They asked, "Why do you have gold and silver in your teeth?" How could I explain cavities and fillings? I didn't have to. There were too many questions:

"Where do you live? Why are you here? Where are your children? Can I have your shoes?"

We talked and laughed for half an hour. I showed them photographs of my daughters and granddaughters. They loved the pictures and several of the braver children asked if they could keep them.

I said it was time I returned to the ceremonial site. "Don't go," they insisted. "Stay and play with us."

I looked at the pleading faces and the big dark eyes of these young boys and girls and knew they were sincere. Not many American women wandered into their territory. "I have to get back to work," I told them. "I have to photograph your friends in the dance ring. Maybe I will get a picture of you when it's your turn to dance." I hoped this would excuse me from our playtime.

As I walked away many of the children followed me, hanging on to my T-shirt or camera bag. I walked swiftly and gradually they drifted off, waving and yelling, "G'day lady, I'll see you later," or "Come back later and play with us." I hoped I would recognize some of them when they danced later.

I felt a tug on my camera bag and looked down. Lydia was still with me. She innocently blinked her big brown eyes and tucked her hand into mine. We walked a short distance together, but I knew I couldn't keep her with me the rest of the day. I reached into my pocket and withdrew a small spiral notebook and a pen. "Do you like to draw pictures?" I asked, kneeling beside her as I drew a sketch of a girl with dark curly hair and a big smile.

She watched me intently. "Would you like to have this notebook to draw pictures of your friends?" I asked as I handed it to her.

She stared at me with a question in her eyes, saying nothing. She was not expecting a gift and wasn't sure if she should accept it. I knew she hadn't been begging and I hoped I hadn't offended her by offering it to her. I said, "It's a gift."

She beamed a smile and gingerly took the paper and pen from my hand. "Thank you, lady," she whispered, as if I had just presented her with a precious jewel. I wished I had more to give her. "Now you can go and make pictures of your friends, just like I did with my camera," I said. She laughed, reached up to squeeze my hand one more time, and quickly ran off in the direction from which we had come. She turned and yelled, "Thank you, lady," one more time and disappeared into the bush.

"Thank you, Lydia," I called back. "Thank you for your beautiful smile."

I reached into my camera bag and retrieved my journal to jot a note:

I have been given a gift today. It is a wonderful memory of life. It is a gesture of peace, a smile of patience, and a gentle breeze of innocence.
The gift is the memory of a little girl named Lydia.

A "swag" is an envelope-type sleeping bag, a "billy" is a kettle on a campfire, a "stubby" is a glass of beer, a "cozzi" is a swimsuit.

"We must have perseverance and, above all, confidence in ourselves. We must believe that we are gifted for something."
— Marie Curie

Children curious about me

Wedgetail eagle

Australia, 1989 · Eagle Dreaming

The rainbow serpent is known to Aboriginal people throughout Australia. In our land, we call him Mundigara. Mundi *means water and* gara *means snake. I've noticed in the Northern Territory they have him in their carvings. In one area his head is shaped like a yam and in another place it is shaped like a kangaroo, so they have different names for him in each area. Each territory has their own names and their own Dreamtime. No matter what he is called, he is known throughout Australia as Creation. The creator of the land and the birds and the animals and of our people. That's what we mean about Dreamtime. — Nola James*

Ocher handprints

Rock art

I was in Northern Queensland, Australia, and had been interviewing the same Aboriginal woman for four days. Each day when Nola and I met, I sat like a hypnotized child listening to her magical stories about Aboriginal ways, Dreamtime, the Rainbow Serpent, crocodiles, birthing babies, totems, and Aboriginal culture, past and present. She said it was important for outsiders to try to understand the heart of her people and their connectedness to the earth. She wanted to preserve her people's culture and wanted their stories recorded before they were forgotten and lost forever.

The three main laws in Aboriginal culture are sharing, caring, and respect. Our people share what they have, care for each other, and respect the elders. Our culture is very old and very sacred.

On the fourth day I sat silently listening to Nola, recording her words. It was late in the afternoon and a beautiful orange sun was slowly slipping into the mountain. Suddenly Nola stopped talking and turned toward me. Her dark deep eyes looked directly into mine. "I have a message for you," she stated. "I know your heart is good and the spirits are guiding you. You must go up into the central mountain region. There you will see a black wedgetail eagle that will fly around you. Do not be afraid. It is welcoming you. Follow it up into the mountain. It has a message for you from the spirits."

I stared at her with a blank look on my face, not knowing what to say. She quietly repeated, "Do not be afraid of going off by yourself. You will be accepted and cared for and you will return safely."

She rested her hand on my shoulder, and her glance met mine with a gentle smile of knowingness. We silently parted as the sun's glow illuminated the mountain into pink, mauve, and magenta.

I went directly to our driver and asked if I could get to the mountain range. "Impossible," he said. "It's hundreds of miles in the opposite direction."

That night I crawled into my swag (sleeping bag), with the star-studded Australian sky as my ceiling. My eyes were wide open with visions of the mountain I could not reach. What was

Woman dancing at corroboree

the meaning of this strange message? The Southern Cross marked my eyelids as I finally found sleep in the early morning hours. And during that time, that Dreamtime, shortly before I awoke, I went to the mountain.

Baby toucan

Peru, 1993 · Amazon Dreaming

A sense of peaceful adventure surrounded me as I entered the untamed world of Amazonia. Walking down a vine-entangled path I came upon a small clearing. A filtered patch of sunlight beamed through the cashapona trees onto the leafy jungle floor. I stopped to breathe in the splendor of this paradise and listen to the melodious songs of hundreds of birds and the constant chatter of monkeys. It was hot, yet sunlight through a window in the thick jungle canopy was inviting.

Suddenly, the jungle stilled. Crickets stopped screeching, birds silenced their songs, and monkeys seemed motionless in the trees. I felt a sharp pain as I was struck from behind. Everything fell into slow motion. Instead of a clean strike, the anaconda was clinging to my leg. Its jaws spread open around my bleeding flesh, clamped like a vise without means or desire to release its grip. I fell to the ground, the musty smells of the forest floor permeated my nostrils, and I lost consciousness.

In an instant my spirit floated upward and I viewed the scene from a few feet above my body. My khaki-clothed form lay within the moist flora of the rain forest floor. Nearby, leaf-cutter ants formed an unbroken line, carrying portions of leaves to their homes. They paid no attention to the fallen giant near their path. The snake, too, lay silent, jaws locked, eyes glaring in a trancelike state. My unconscious mind calmly took control and commanded the snake to release its grip and leave. It was not a roaring command. It was an unspoken voice of authority. Of power.

Sixteen-foot anaconda

The anaconda, eyes still glazed, released its mighty grip and slowly slithered into the green wall of jungle, as if obeying a superior being.

My spirit hovered over my body for a time, sending healing energy into the wounded leg. Spirit passed a hand of light over the leg and the wound disappeared. Then spirit re-entered my body. I became conscious, sat up, and watched the last link of slithering snake body disappear into the bushes. Without any fear or questioning of what had just happened, I rose and continued on my way, as if I had just experienced a common occurrence.

The Achuara shaman looked at me. His intense black eyes fixed on mine as I finished telling him about my dream. His tanned, weathered face was serious as he pondered what I had just told him. He spoke Achuara and Spanish, I spoke only English. My jungle guide, José, interpreted. "When did you have this dream?" he asked.

"Just three nights before coming to the Amazon," I responded.

"Were you afraid?"

I said, "No."

Baby caiman

"Energy creates energy."
— Sarah Bernhardt

▽▽▽▽▽▽▽▽▽▽▽▽▽▽▽▽▽▽▽▽▽▽▽▽▽▽▽▽▽▽▽▽▽▽▽▽▽▽▽

A chicken that we named "lunch"

He questioned me further, "Are you afraid now that you are here?"

Again my answer was "No."

He nodded, said "Good," then lowered his head and continued carving shavings from an *ajo-sacha* (false garlic) vine.

Silence. I kept looking at José for a sign of what to do. Was this the answer I had walked miles through the jungles of Peru to find? José sat quietly, watching the shaman shave medicine from the vine into a gourd bowl. Sensing my impatience, José filled in the silence explaining that the shaman was making an important medicine mixture for a healing he would do in our camp tonight for a man with asthma. The shaman said prayers while he worked with the plants. More silence. Finally he spoke.

"Have you had other dreams like this?"

"No, but I did have a dream that I was supposed to look for some sort of medicine stick on this trip. Was the snake my medicine stick?" I asked.

Shavings from the trunk of the yanahuarango tree can be cooked with cupati vine as a contraceptive. Drunk for three to four nights, it lasts for three to four years. If drunk for ten consecutive nights, its contraceptive effects may be permanent.

"Keep things on your trip in perspective, and you'll be amazed at the perspective you'll gain on things back home."

— Gain Rubin Bereny

Achuara mother and child

The shaman's wife

I traded T-shirts, fish line, fishing hooks, flashlights, and batteries for blowguns, crude jewelry, pottery, wood utensils, baskets, and chambira palm bags.

"No," he answered.

He went back to his shavings. Silence. I waited. Finally the shaman rose, dusted off his trousers, and said, "When I come to your camp tonight I will make a ceremony for you. We will find out about this medicine stick and your dreams." Then he walked away.

▼   ▼   ▼

I could hear him in the distance, singing and chanting as he worked with the asthmatic man. I sat on my sleeping bag, inside my mosquito net enclosure, writing in my journal, anxiously awaiting my turn. The blackness of the night engulfed the *tambo*, which was raised on stilts above the ground to accommodate the dry and wet seasons of the Amazon. Candles and kerosene lanterns dimly lit the camp.

Using a blowgun, it takes three darts soaked in cuare to fell a monkey. If you don't have the cuare plant nearby, you can make a mixture of isulu ants, ayahuasca, and toe plant.

Finally, I heard the creak of crude floorboards as the shaman and José followed the walkway leading toward me. Their shadows loomed like dinosaurs on the loose weave of my mosquito netting. We cordially nodded heads toward each other and then sat in a triangle around a single candle. The shaman chanted and sang in low whispers, whistled through his teeth, and made motions with his hands. He rolled black tobacco into a leaf and blew smoke all around me. He handed me a smooth amber colored stone, his healing stone, telling me to rub it on my body and hold it in my hand. It would absorb my energy. Then he read the stone.

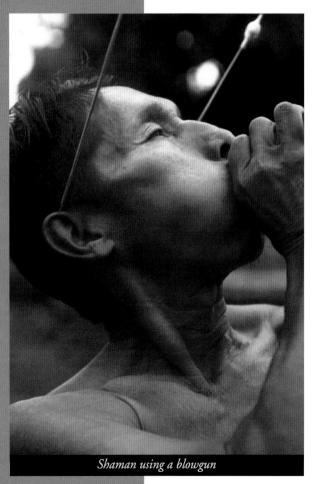

Shaman using a blowgun

This medicine man sprinkled *ajo-sacha* into his gourd bowl, tossed in a handful of black tobacco, mashed in sugarcane root and yucca, and mixed it all together with other roots and herbs. To this he added river water and then handed it to me to drink. I reluctantly took a sip and nearly gagged. It was bad. He continued blowing smoke and chanting and every once in a while stopped and handed me the gourd to take another drink. He kept asking me if I was dizzy or had to throw up. Although the "potion" tasted terrible, it wasn't nauseating. I said "No."

The ceremony continued and I wondered if his goal was to make me keep drinking until I was sick. I prayed he wouldn't make me finish drinking the entire thing. "Am I supposed to vomit?" I finally asked.

"Vomiting gets rid of dark and evil spirits and poisons in the body," he explained. He was pleased that I didn't have to vomit. It meant that I was free of illness and dark spirits.

The ceremony lasted an hour and a half and ended with a healing ritual, summoning the spirits to protect me. The shaman told me that in a few nights I would dream again and he would interpret that dream to give me the answers I was looking for. He added, "If anyone tries to give you a gift, you should accept it. No matter what it is. Accept it. It is important."

I simply nodded. He turned and walked quietly into the deep darkness of the jungle night.

The taste of black tobacco stained my mouth and throat and I could not swallow it away. I did not dream that night.

▼ ▼ ▼

We were on a three-day jungle survival trip up a small tributary of the Blanquillo River. We had literally chopped our way through trees and vines that appeared as the river level dropped. "The trees cry when I come to the river!" the shaman called, swinging his machete. It had taken us nearly two days to travel what normally took three hours. Along the way the shaman called to birds in the thick rain forest and they answered his call. He shouted to the monkeys and after a short time we heard crashing noises through the trees. An entire clan of rare Uakari monkeys responded to his call and came with curiosity to see what we looked like. They hung around, swinging overhead, answering the hoots and grunts of the shaman. Then they noisily returned the way they had come.

Our guide pointed out jaguar, ocelot, tapir, and anteater tracks along the river bank. I watched while the shaman's trained eyes patiently stared into the water. He aimed carefully and threw a crude handmade spear into the muddy river and came up with a fish every time. I could not see anything in the black water, no bubbles, no ripples, only black river water. How could his eyes be so sharp?

Later in the day, Achuco, our boatman, pointed to a small inlet. We paddled toward the bank for a better look. Coiled among the fresh, flowing water was a huge anaconda. The snake was at least twelve inches around with eyes the size of quarters. It was soothing itself with a

The shaman drinking yucca mix

▼▼

massage of swift water flowing into the river. The shaman got out of the boat and edged toward the anaconda. The snake didn't move.

The shaman looked up at me. "Is this the anaconda in your dream?" he asked.

"This one is much larger," I replied.

"Are you afraid?" he asked. I was surprised at my calm. All I could think about was how beautiful it was, all shiny and glistening with the sunlight playing on the water over its back. "No," I answered.

He reached for a stick and poked the snake gently. It uncoiled, and slowly slithered into the river, right next to our boat. The snake was over 16 feet long. Achuco estimated it weighed 80 to 100 pounds and noted that it had survived to grow so big because we were in a little-traveled area of the jungle. Natives rarely come here. An electric eel flashed by our boat.

▼ ▼ ▼

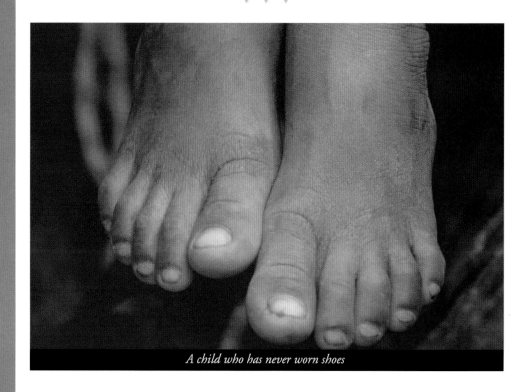

A child who has never worn shoes

"In order to live freely and happily you must sacrifice boredom. It is not always an easy sacrifice."

— Anonymous

As darkness invaded we sparingly used flashlights to find our way upriver. My senses were filled with the sounds and smells of the jungle. Hundreds of species of tree frogs chorused, roared, and sang throughout the night. At one point the shaman directed me to shine my light into the water. His keen eye concentrated for several minutes and suddenly he reached into the depths and snatched out a four-foot baby caiman from the splashing water. The gator's eyes reflected the beam of light from my flashlight as it wiggled and wrenched to free itself. *"Cumpashin!"* the shaman proudly yelled, *"Cumpashin!"* This translates roughly as "What a good friend am I." He held it tightly so I could touch its leathery skin and then gently released it back into the water.

A few yards upriver we paddled close to a bushy fallen tree. The shaman slowly reached out and, making soothing hissing-like noises, slipped his hand under a small sleeping bird. There it sat, perched on his finger, sound asleep. He touched its head, still making lullaby noises, and gently replaced it on its branch.

We finally set up a makeshift camp, clearing an area with machetes to hang our mosquito netting. Recalling the anaconda, caiman, and animal tracks we

Young girl in Amazon jungle

dark. "We must be there before dark," Achuco urged. "Snakes come out onto the trails at night and it could be very dangerous," he warned. The very thought kept my adrenaline flowing and my feet moving.

▼   ▼   ▼

Sitting around the campfire that night, I listened to the shaman. He told of when he first began his shamanic journey. He stared into the fire as he described a dream he had when a beautiful woman appeared and said she would take care of him.

"She represents the spirit of the plants and she guides me in knowing how to prepare for healing," he revealed. "The chanting during my ceremonies is prayers of thanks and requests for additional guidance. We must always remember to thank the plants and the spirits."

We sat silently, watching the flames of the fire dance into the night.

"I had a dream last night," I announced. He didn't answer, just looked at me, waiting for me to continue. The black pupils of his eyes seemed to catch light from the campfire as they directed their gaze to me. "I was in a dugout canoe on the river. The water was smooth and clear, yet the river was very foggy. Suddenly another dugout canoe appeared out of the mist. In it was a sparsely dressed native man with long, dark hair and a serious look on his face. He paddled up to my canoe, reached out, and handed a beautiful bird-of-paradise flower to me. I slowly reached out and accepted the plant. He smiled and paddled away, disappearing into the fog."

The shaman stared at me for what seemed to be forever, shadows of the campfire playing on his thin brown face. I returned his gaze. Finally he spoke. "You accepted the gift?"

I said, "Yes."

"Good," he replied. "It is a good dream. The flower is your medicine stick. You must use it."

Silence.

"But what does it mean?" I asked. "How do I use it?"

Silence.

Isulu ants and drowning are the major causes of childhood death in the Amazon jungle.

Child in jungle village

▼▼▼

"You will understand the meaning of your dream when you are ready to accept the answer," he said firmly.

He reached over and retrieved his gourd of yucca mixture, taking a long drink. Then he motioned it toward me. "What is in it?" I asked, wondering if it was the same concoction he had used during my healing ceremony.

"It is what I drink to summon the spirits into my head to ask for answers in my healing." He pushed the gourd into my hands. "Drink," he said.

I looked at José. He nodded his head. "It is an honor seldom offered," José whispered. I accepted the gourd and took a drink of the sour mystical formula. Tasting the terrible black tobacco burning down my throat, I tried not to make a face. I smiled and handed the gourd back, offering a weak "Thank you." When the shaman finished the drink he handed me his empty gourd bowl.

"Keep this," he said simply. "It is for you to use."

He grabbed a branch and began to stir the campfire. Wild red flames snapped, reaching high into the Amazon sky. He stood watching them swirling upward, burning themselves out. Their embers disappeared into blackness. The shaman turned to me and smiled.

"It is a good dream," he repeated. "A good dream."

Three-toed sloth

It is said that to come to Machu Picchu (Quechua for "old pcak") on the Inca Trail, the path taken by the last Incas, is the same as reaching heaven and looking God in the face.

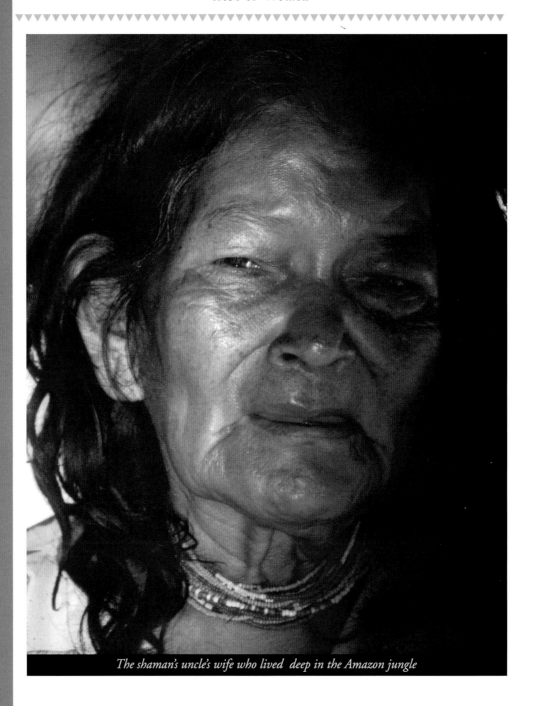

The shaman's uncle's wife who lived deep in the Amazon jungle

Peru, 1994 · Center of the Swarm

I sat on the rough bamboo flooring of a *tambo* in the dense primary forest along the Blanquijo River, a tributary of the mighty Amazon River. Our small group of three photographers, boatman, guide, and shaman were on a three-day jungle survival trip and were preparing for our return trip to camp. We planned to float downriver during the night hours, hoping to see tapir, jaguars, and other mammals come to the water to drink. It sounded a little daring, but very exciting.

As I sat writing in my journal I suddenly heard the loud buzzing of bees ascending upon us. The drone grew louder and louder. I looked up from my pages to see a thick cloud of large black bees flying all around me. I glanced over at Ramone, the shaman, and he motioned for me to be still.

"They won't sting you," José translated. "Just be very still."

At this point I realized that I was the only person being swarmed by the bees. I could hear shrieking in the distance. José again called out in a very steady voice, "Don't be afraid. They can sense your fear. Just be very still, they won't hurt you." Both he and Ramone were sitting and calmly watching me.

I closed my mouth tightly and took in long, slow breaths through my nose, trying to squeeze my nostrils together as much as I could. I squinted so bees wouldn't get into my eyes, behind my sunglasses. My sweat bandanna covered my ears and I was grateful to be wearing a long-sleeved shirt, long pants, socks, and tennis shoes. My shirt sleeves were rolled up to my elbows and I could see my arms nearly covered with bees. They crawled, moving their feelers to test my skin. It tickled. I sat still and couldn't believe my calm. I was literally covered by hundreds of bees, perhaps thousands, and I was not getting stung. Just as incredible, I was actually calmly sitting and observing the swarm! I totally trusted Ramone and José's confident assurance that if I did not show fear I would not be hurt.

I began to feel like I was a part of the swarm. I was one of them. I was at their core. They were landing and flying all around me, yet I was strangely peaceful. I was accepted by them as simply another part of nature. I felt like I was the queen bee gathering her swarm around her for a reunion. I lost all track of time.

Gradually the bees started to leave. First a few flew away and then, as though a

"You must do the things you think you cannot do."

— Eleanor Roosevelt

whistle had been blown, the rest flew. The music of their buzz distanced into the jungle. I wanted to shout after them and thank them — for what, I'm not sure, but somehow I felt this experience was a gift of nature.

Sitting still while the last straggler took flight, I looked back at Ramone and José. They were just nodding and smiling. I felt like I had just passed some huge test of the jungle, a mystical shamanic initiation.

I nodded back at them, looked off in the direction the bees had flown, and calmly returned to writing in my journal as if being swarmed by bees was an everyday occurrence. Perhaps in the Amazon jungle it is.

Green parrot snake

Local natives resting after performing a friendship dance for us

▼▼

Turkey, 1991 · Behind the Veil

The city of Ezurum lay silent in traditional afternoon rest. I followed the cobbled path of a shaded street photographing brightly painted doors and tattered curtains blowing gently in the autumn breeze. Shopkeepers relaxed on straight-backed chairs, gazing out windows while they drank their tea. Water in hookahs boiled for their daily smoke. Men things.

Suddenly she appeared in the corner of my lens, standing solid against shadows of a mud wall. Draped women in Turkey usually flee or turn their heads away so photographs can't be made. But she faced me, like a dead-end alley. She wanted — challenged — me to make a picture.

Her eyes said, "Now. Quickly."

I raised my camera and nodded a "yes," just to be sure. She bowed in return.

Zoom in, click, click, click.

Only three shots.

She blinked as if to say, "Thank you," turned quickly and disappeared into the shadows.

Gone before any man noticed her consent.

Woman in Ezurum

Women drape differently in each area of Turkey

Going to the well for water

Women washing wool at river

▼▼▼

Turkey, 1991 · In the Shadow of Mount Ararat

I traveled to Turkey in 1991 with a team of photographers planning to climb Mount Ararat in search of Noah's Ark. Our climbing permits didn't arrive in time, so instead we spent four days photographing the women and families in some of the small villages surrounding the mountain. The entire time I felt a strong sense of feminine energy calling to me. Mount Ararat could be seen everywhere we went, looming like a mother over the land. She was hypnotizing. I could not help but look at her longingly every day. One afternoon I walked into a field and sat among the wildflowers. The mountain spoke to me. This is what she said:

Village at the foot of Mount Ararat

Group of women in a small Kurdish village near Van

I am the mighty Mount Ararat. You are invited, my friends, to visit with me. You tickle me with the pointed spikes of your crampons as you climb my summit and keep me company. I listen as your excited voices echo through my valleys while you argue over the secrets tucked within my folds. It's the Ark of Noah you seek . . . this secret hidden deep within my very soul.

But why do you seek the ark? What would you do if you found it?

Haji woman who had journeyed to Mecca

Build an altar and show reverence for this man Noah and his family because they obeyed without question? Give thanks because the earth was cleared of all impurities and was offered another chance to redeem herself? Worship the Ark itself as a symbol of faith and endurance and as a sign of hope and peace? Would you respect me with my pristine cliffs and treacherous glacial crevices and keep me free of heavily trodden paths, concrete highways, and commercial houses? Would you honor the very earth that lies within my shell of boulders and snowcapped peaks and not leave signs of litter in your wake as you rush tourists to see this Ark?

Would you still stand in awe and watch as the wind blows clouds over my lofty peaks, while sunlight glistens off the streaked fingers of snow, racing down my slopes?

I think not.

I think you would argue over my borders and sink your picks into the very flesh of my soul in search of ways to seek profit from my hidden treasures. You would take them from me, piece by piece, boasting that you were here. You would say I have surrendered, that I have given up my possessions of five thousand years, and that I have lost my mystery.

"So many moments, all so simple. God, do I love it here on earth!"

— Fannie Gaynes

"Can't you hear the voice of wisdom? She is standing at the city gates and at every fork in the road and at the door of every house. Listen to what she says . . . 'I, wisdom, give good advice and common sense. I love all who love me. Those who search for me shall surely find me.'"

— Proverbs 8: 1–3, 14,17, *The Living Bible*

Kurdish girl

test your strength and endurance and your faith. And then say *"Gule Gule"* as you leave in exhaustion and pain, knowing that as you pass by you will always look back and still long for me with teary emotion.

I know you will return. For you see, even if I give up my treasure, you will find that it is really me, Mount Ararat, Agri Dagi, that you long for. Not the Ark of Noah.

The lessons to be learned along the way are in the journey itself, not in the journey's end.

Sunset on Lake Van

Namibia, Africa, 1996 · Himba – Clay People

Himba woman

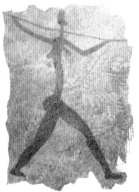

We had driven for days through the bush, not always on roads, but along dry riverbeds, over hills, and into sand gullies. Wayne, my bush guide, seemed to have a map in his head. He drew dotted lines on my wrinkled Namibia map highlighting the new trail we were blazing. I was amazed at his sense of direction in the vast wilderness of Kaokoland. We were searching for a nomadic Himba tribe and the rare desert elephant. Out of approximately seventy remaining desert elephants on the Skeleton Coast, we encountered eight — very good.

We had met Ova Himba tribal people in the small "village"

Instead of bone, they sometimes make bracelets from PVC pipe

If you are lost in Namibia, find a comiphora tree. The bark is lighter and shiny on the exposed side, and the exposed side is true north.

There are three styles of hair. One means the girl is an adolescent, another that she has reached puberty and can marry, and the third is a goat-skinned headpiece worn on the top of the head, showing the woman is married.

Hair wrapped in clay

of Puros and in an area where the natives had built semipermanent mud huts. They were waiting for the outside world to reach them — ready to sell their wares, such as handmade doll replicas, necklaces carved from macalani palm, and "ivory" bracelets now made from PVC pipe.

Locating true nomadic Himba, however, was more difficult. We had been searching for a few days and most unexpectedly, in the isolation of the bush, a woman appeared, walking on a dry riverbed among camel thorn trees. Our path seemed to have led us directly to her. This Himba woman stood tall, head held high while her red ocher skin glimmered in the sunlight.

She walked toward us, bare feet clinging to the dust of the outback. Balanced perfectly on her head was a heavy milking pot. She was accompanied by another woman, a man, and a goat. At first, the goat dangled from her hand like a rag mop. I thought the animal was dead, but as we approached she flipped it up into the crook of her arm and cradled it like a baby. It bleated in defense or gratefulness.

Crushing red ocher and nursing baby

Himba woman and goat in the bush

She looked directly at me with an expression that challenged me to respond to her. I smiled and said simply "Hello." I didn't speak Himba. I didn't speak Afrikaans either. Wayne spoke English, German, Swahili, and Afrikaans. He asked permission in Afrikaans to photograph. She didn't know about cameras; it didn't matter to her. Wayne continued to speak to them as I photographed.

Traditionally, Himba women are bare breasted, wear furry goatskin skirts, riveted ankle and arm bracelets, and carved bone necklaces. They are covered from head to foot with clay, red ocher to moisturize and protect their bronze skin from the hot sun. The style of their hair depicts the status of their womanhood: puberty, ready for a husband, or married.

We gave this Himba woman and her companions sustainable gifts of water, sugar, and fruit. But I felt the gift was really mine — a brief exchange with a tribal nomadic woman, living a simple life in the bush, one with the elements of nature, walking respectfully upon the earth.

Free. Until civilization reaches her and demands change.

Herero mother and child walking in Botswana

Herero woman, Botswana

"I was once asked if I'd like to meet the president of a certain country. I said, 'No. But I'd love to meet some sheepherders.'"

— James Michener

Making beads in jewelry factory, Nairobi, Kenya

Egypt, Africa, 1994 · In the Eye of Cheops

The brooding figure of the Great Sphinx, guardian of mystical places, cast a long shadow in the dry shifting desert sands that edged the west bank of the Nile. In front of me loomed the Great Pyramid of Cheops, a stone monument that soon swallowed me up as I entered and followed the stairway tunnel of the grand gallery that led to the king's chamber. The room itself represents the conquering of death by life; the victory of wisdom over ignorance. It is sometimes referred to as the Room of Judgment and Purification of the Nations.

I stubbornly carried my thirty-five-pound camera bag as I climbed, bent over in the low gallery. Sweating and gasping for air, I finally entered the chamber room. I stood breathless and peered inside the dimly lit burial chamber of the pharaoh Khufu, later known by the Greek name of Cheops. To my surprise, a group of people had formed a

Camel ride at 4:00 A.M. in Cheops

A family in Luxor

circle in the center of the room. At my right, encrusted into the ground, were the remains of the open, empty, red granite sarcophagus, placed in a north-south direction. The rest of the chamber was gray, stone cold, and barren except for the colorful circle of mortals. I immediately felt a wind of energy swirl around me. It brought my attention to the circle. One woman, dressed in white, was standing in the center as the others held hands around her. They were chanting and praying. I set my camera bag against the stone of the cold chamber floor and joined the circle. The lady in the center nodded, welcoming me with her smile. My hands were uplifted by people on each side and I became a part of an unbroken link of prayer.

My eyes swept the circle. About fifteen men and women of different cultures and colors encircled the Spanish-speaking woman. Their eyes were shut and she approached them individually, chanting and praying. They answered her in Spanish or their own tongue, concluding with what I understood to be "Amen." I couldn't translate all the words, but the language of peace and love spoke loudly. Many of the people began to cry. Tears of joy and contentment silently rolled down their cheeks.

Then it was my turn. I closed my eyes and the woman in white, with straight, long black hair and deep brown eyes, gently put her hand on my forehead. I was still breathing heavily from the climb and knew I was sweating. Her hand didn't flinch from my sweaty brow. She prayed in a fluid language that was music to my ears. Her hand moved to my chest and my breathing immediately calmed. A small miracle. I was breathing normally and my forehead was dry. I felt the peace and love I had seen emitting from the other links of this circle. "Amen," I responded, knowing that whatever she prayed for me was the right thing. Light flowed into me, down through my right hand on to the next person.

Too soon, the ritual was over and the circle broke into small hugs of people. The Spanish woman approached, embraced me, and spoke. A turbaned man standing nearby translated in broken English that she was thanking me for coming. She was thanking me! Didn't she know that she was the gift? I thanked her for the prayers and for her "healing." She calmly smiled, the brown and blue of our eyes mixing together as they penetrated deep from a source within each of us. Then she was swallowed into the crowd with a hug from a black man dressed in an African caftan.

I discovered that the "circle" started with a religious group from Mexico that traveled to Egypt on a pilgrimage. As this group sang and prayed in the chambers, others, like me, reached the top of the long staircase and felt compelled to join in. There was no difference in culture, no "one" religion, no need for common language, no gender. We were all children of the Universe. The empty sarcophagus and king's chamber were a church for a unity of souls that left an energy ring of peace for others to enter.

Here, in the vastness of the Sahara Desert, the oneness of the universe glowed in a light beam of human

> "Realize that we truly are one. We may be different in our cultures, color, beliefs, sizes, shapes, morals, and education, but we have the same feelings of wanting to be loved, accepted, and safe. We want our families and children to be healthy and safe and happy. We all need love in our lives."
>
> — Anonymous

beings forming a white circle of peace in the great chamber of the mighty pyramid of Cheops. I was mesmerized as I reluctantly found my way through the grand gallery leading down to the doorway that would brought me back outside into the world.

My life had been touched by an overwhelming feeling of "one" in the mystical eye of the Great Pyramid of Egypt.

King Tut's mask

Women at Luxor posing with me

Traditional wedding costume worn in Morocco

▼▼▼▼▼▼▼▼▼▼▼▼▼▼▼▼▼▼▼▼▼▼▼▼▼▼▼▼▼▼▼▼▼▼▼▼▼▼▼

Tanzania, Africa, 1994 · To Celebrate Womanhood

A young girl waiting to be circumcised

In some places on this earth it is a celebration, a rite of passage, when a girl becomes a woman. Her youthful body has reached puberty. The straight hips and flat chest begin to round and shape themselves into the soft flesh that will grow into a mature, desirable woman. It is a time for her young woman body to bleed for its birthright, a time for its own cycle of life to begin.

She must step into her place in the world and announce that she is truly a woman.

She is ripe.

She can bear her own children.

Masai women in Africa are celebrated. This thirteen-year-old woman wears rings on all her fingers and toes. Her hair is beaded and decorated.

She is being honored by her family today. She is proud.

Tomorrow she will be circumcised.

"Why?" I ask, appalled at the very thought of this ritual.

Her mother replies, "She will be cut so she won't have orgasms, or feel pleasure during sex. She will be cut so she won't wander in lust... like a man."

A celebration?

The hands and feet of the village witch doctor

When the women dance,
their wide beaded necklaces
bounce up and down to
the beat of their clapsticks.

Masai jewelry

Masai woman

Masai place heavy copper weights in their ears when they are young. This stretches the earlobe, which is a mark of beauty to them.

Masai woman in Tanzania

Masai teens with Town & Country *magazine in Tanzania*

Kuna woman smoking her pipe

San Blas Islands, Panama, 1990 · Island Paradise

I flew in to Punta Pitia airport on the capital island of El Porvenir, which translates as "the future," and was shuttled by boat to nearby Wichub-Huala Island. The archipelagos that form the San Blas Islands are made of 365 small islands that dot a long narrow space between the Caribbean Sea and the Continental Divide. Tourists to the islands are rare.

I swung, lazily, in a hammock under the woven grasses of a *pillapa*, sipping Colombian coffee, as I watched mothers and daughters concentrating on their *mola* making. They were sewing tiny stitches in colorful layered fabric. This is a long tradition of the Kuna Indians of the San Blas Islands.

Mother and daughter sewing molas

There is a long history behind the art of *mola* designs. Today, birds, turtles, and iguanas replace the wide geometric patterns crafted by Kuna grandmothers. During World War II, *mola* motifs represented replicas of billboards, can labels, cigarette packages, and advertisements that women saw on cloth-purchasing trips to Panama or Colombia. *Molas* that hung on fences and palm branches in this village were of the same bright colors that ancestors had used, but the designs changed from geometric to much earthier themes with fish, crab, and snake motifs.

Women and girls not only made *molas*, they also wore traditional *mola* clothing. Two *molas* were sewn together to form a blouse, with front and back patterns always being different. A skirt was made by wrapping a piece of cloth around the body and tucking the end in at the waist. It was worn over a short, solid-colored underskirt, known as a *picha makkalet*.

When the skirt began to fade or wear, the women cut it up into a pattern to make a new *mola*. Nothing was wasted. If a woman grew tired of wearing the same blouse, she simply took it apart and sold the squares to a tourist market on the mainland. Panama and Colombia were hours away by boat, or twenty-five minutes via a daily ten-passenger plane that carried supplies to the islands.

Head scarves, nose rings, and beaded jewelry were everyday wear for the Kuna women. In keeping with tradition, a narrow black line, stained by berry juice,

Kuna elder

Children with pet parrots

was drawn down the nose to ward off evil spirits. Other decorations included long strings of small glass trade beads which were wound into wide arm and ankle bracelets with geometric lines designed into the pattern.

Preparing food was a long, drawn-out process as grains were spread out to dry in the sun after being pounded and crushed with crude wooden mallets and hollowed-out tree vessels. I watched a woman fill a calabash with water from a deep hole in the island as she prepared for our meal of fresh fish, lobster, and crab, an everyday menu for island inhabitants.

There were no modern cooking appliances on these islands, yet there was a gas-fueled generator that ran each evening. It was used to power electricity for the island's one television set that was turned on for three hours each evening. Men, women, and children gathered under the open sky to watch news from the mainland, and the show *Dallas*.

▼▼

Along with freshly caught crab and lobster, we ate rice, mangos, coconuts, pineapples, and bananas.

Medicine men in the Kuna community are highly revered and are called *inatuledis.* They work with herbs, smoke, and chanting.

I sat back and soaked in this island paradise with conch shells lining the white sandy beach, palm trees swaying in the breeze, and the sound of gentle waves slapping against dugout canoes. In the distance, women were dancing and singing to the music of reed flutes — and under the starry moonlit night of the Caribbean sky, natives sat and watched television.

from school. I reached over and squeezed her hand. She looked at me and nodded. I understood her anguish. She admitted she was torn by loyalty for her family, the loss they felt, and the hatred they harbored for the United States government that was responsible for all the death and destruction. Yet she had to consider her own survival — a job — that today required her to act as a guide for Americans who wanted to photograph the remains of Noriega's command headquarters, the graveyard of a neighborhood. She was very forgiving. "It's not your fault," she said, responding to the man who called us killers.

"I know," I replied. "Sometimes it's hard to be an American too."

It is almost 3:00 A.M. and I'm still unable to sleep. I rest the pen on my journal and look out the window into the noisy city. Neon signs light the night sky and a billboard across the street reflects its colors, with words that proudly proclaim, "Mi nombre es Panamá" — My name is Panama.

Mother and baby in the church at Portabelo

Children of Belize

Belize, 1990 · The Bush Doctor's Apprentice

"I give thanks to the spirit of this plant and have faith with all my heart that this plant will cure the sickness of the people," I prayed over and over as I picked fresh *cordonsillo*, pheasant tail, *cruxi*, and *anal* leaves in the rainforest of Belize.

Dr. Rosita Arvigo said the prayer first in Spanish and then translated it into English for me to memorize. "Before gathering medicine, we always give thanks to the spirit of the plant and to the earth, whose child the plant is," she said. Her teacher, Don Elijio Panti, taught her that faith is the most important tool in healing and that prayers were an essential part of the healing process.

Rosita and her family homesteaded Ix Chel Farm in the Cayo district of Belize in the early 1980s. Ix Chel is named for the Mayan goddess of medicine, weaving, childbirth, rainbows, and the moon. Nestled within the boundaries of their thirty-five acre farm is nature's own pharmacy, alive with hundreds of medicinal plants and herbs that grow native to the jungle.

Mayan bush doctor Don Elijio Panti was known as *"el mero,"* the authentic one, the most well-known bush doctor in all Central America. He had been a good teacher to Rosita. It had taken a long time for her to gain the trust he demanded to become an apprentice. She, after all, was not Mayan. She was not even from Belize. She was an American and she was a woman.

The crystal Don Elijio Panti found on his doorstep after a dream

▼▼▼▼▼▼▼▼▼▼▼▼▼▼▼▼▼▼▼▼▼▼▼▼▼▼▼▼▼▼▼▼▼▼▼▼▼▼

*"The Lord formed me in
the beginning, before she
created anything else.
From ages past, I am.
I existed before the earth
began. I lived before
the oceans were created,
before the springs
bubbled forth their waters
onto the earth; before
the mountains and the
hills were made.
I was always at her side
like a little child. I was her
constant delight, laughing
and playing in her pres-
ence. And how happy I
was with what she cre-
ated — her wide world
and all her family of
mankind."*

*— Adapted from
Proverbs 22–28 and
30–31, The Living Bible*

Duties of a bush doctor were not taken lightly. It required being a doctor, priest, shaman, *curandero* (healer), snake doctor, household healer, midwife, pharmacist, bone setter, and *sobadero* (massage therapist). The job also required believing in the unbelievable, the voices of spirits.

Don Elijio accepted Rosita as his student and she worked alongside him, learning to heal with the earth. She was also introduced to the nine Mayan spirits who rule over the Central American people. These are the spirits who make the winds blow, the plants grow, the rains come, the sun shine, and the wild animals lay down their lives for the hunter. "The spirits are the right hand of God," Don Elijio told her.

After years of studying with Don Elijio, a *Primicia*, an ancient Mayan ceremony for prayer and thanksgiving, was performed for Rosita. Don Elijio gave offerings of flowers, first fruits, a candle for each of the four directions, and nine gourd bowls of *atole,* or corn mush, on a handmade stick-and-palm altar. During the ceremony he used leaves of the *tzib che* plant for cleansing and protection from the force of spirits that would come to receive the offerings. He burned sacred *copal* resin incense, chanted a special Mayan prayer called a *cantico*, and asked the spirits to give Rosita, his beloved apprentice, every consideration they gave to him and to please respond to her every request for help.

This was important. If a shaman didn't know how to heal someone, he relied on the spirits to guide him, waiting for a dream vision where he would be shown the plant

Chopping bark for medicine

▼▼▼

and told the dosage and treatment. The spirits were wise counselors. Don Elijio asked that Rosita receive dream visions so she might draw from their wisdom as she healed people in good faith.

I was honored to visit Rosita's farm and walk with her along the Panti Trail to hear about the healing properties of jungle plants. "Nature does not create a problem without knowing about both its dangers and its healing plants," she stated. She talked about the "doctrine of signature," a system where plants offer clues to their usefulness by color, shape, and growth. She showed me a medicinal vine with a "cross" on it, a symbol of healing formed by the stem and leaves. Red in plants and berries often indicates remedies useful to the blood. The textbook was in Rosita's head. She had learned her lessons well.

We picked healing herbs for Don Elijio. At ninety-plus it was getting difficult for him to go to his jungle pharmacy to collect medicine. When we arrived in his village he was sitting on a stump of wood, chopping bark with a machete. He wore trousers, a long-sleeved white shirt, and a baseball cap. His thick, dark-rimmed glasses kept slipping down his nose. He received our gift of healing leaves and invited us into his thatched-roofed hut.

In return for our gift he offered to make a ceremony. He asked my name as he took out a marble-like crystal he called a *sastun*. *Sas* means "light" and *tun* is "stone." He placed it in a small pottery vase and rolled it around nine times on his oilcloth table as he whistled and chanted a Mayan prayer of blessing. Then he had me hold the *sastun* in my right hand and shake it like dice. I slowly opened my hand, with my palm flat, and the light from the open door shone through the crystal marble. He closely examined the *sastun* to see the position of the floating bubbles around the stationary ones inside. This "reading" told

Rosita Arvigo on the Panti Trail medicine walk

> "I want to be all that I am capable of becoming."
> — Katherine Mansfield

> "It is not the easy or convenient life for which I search . . . but life lived to the edge of all my possibility."
> — Anonymous

Woman staying with Rosita for a healing

him if there were bad spirits around me. If he saw darkness he would have to do a purification ritual. He was pleased; there were no bad spirits.

Don Elijio asked if I had something I wanted blessed. I took off the crystal necklace I had purchased in Australia and put it on his table along with photographs of my children. Tears welled up in my eyes as I stood and watched him working with his *sastun*, blessing my belongings with chanting and singing. I felt so much warmth and love for this giving, caring man I had just met. No wonder the spirits had chosen to protect him and guide him with his work.

Standing at my side, Rosita noticed my emotions and gently put an understanding hand on my shoulder. Her eyes beamed with pride as she watched her teacher, this Mayan bush doctor in the remote jungle, performing his healing work.

Rosita understood better than anyone how important Don Elijio's work was. For his magic was also hers.

Don Elijio Panti died in 1997.

Now all his healing magic belongs to Rosita.

Nepal, 1994 · Nagi Gompa Monastery

She lingered in shadows of black, gray, and maroon. A halo of light was her only guide as she walked through musty hallways where thick walls and worn wooden doors share the whisper of nuns. Her small hands held an offering of golden marigolds. Yellow — holy color of the gods.

She was a child in a monastery of nuns. Ten years old, no longer an orphan alone but a sibling with many sisters, a daughter with many mothers, one of a family of hundreds. She was a Buddhist *ani* living in the clouds on a mountaintop with a heavenly view over the great city of Kathmandu.

▼ ▼ ▼

Ten-year-old ani

Cleaning prayer wheels at Boudenath Stupa

Nuns at Nagi Gompa

"Work, pray, practice," said the *ani*'s teacher.

"But what is practice?" I asked.

"You must practice to understand yourself," replied the Lama. "Sit quietly and contemplate. Get to know your anger, your fear, all your emotions. Dissect them and speak with them. Accept yourself and know every part of your own being. To understand oneself is to have compassion for everything."

▼   ▼   ▼

The little *ani* and I walked down the mountain to the city to buy shoes. She slipped out of her too-small rubber sandals into a new pair, carefully counted forty-five rupees (less than one U.S. dollar) into the shopkeeper's hand, and walked away.

"Wait!" I called, as I reached for the discarded shoes. "You've forgotten your old sandals."

She glanced back at me, "No, leave them," she firmly replied. "I only need one pair. Leave them for someone who has none."

Compassion.

I must practice.

Prayer flags blowing in the wind

A *saddhu* is a
Hindu holy man.

A *baba* is a holy man.

Woman in Himalayas

Woman in Kathmandu

A girl and her goat

Stringing marigolds in Gandruk

▼▼

*"Take time in your life —
no matter how busy —
to honor the beauty of
life around you. Smile at
a flower, answer a bird,
talk to a tree and tell it
you know it's holding
centuries of 'seeing.'
Ask permission before
you pick up stones and
feathers and flowers.
Respect everything
around you. Look
at other men and
women and see
yourself in them."*

— Anonymous

Girl on Himalayan trek

Washing dishes at a community water source

"Woman is the creator of
the universe,
the universe is her form.
Woman is the foundation
of the world.
She is the true form
of the body,
whatever form she takes,
whether the form of a
man or a woman."

— Saktisangama Tantra

The oldest living woman in Nepal, according to locals

Woman spreading grain to dry

The red tikka powder in her scalp means she is married

A young woman at Agra who gave me a flower

India, 1994 · Namaste

"Namaste," she shyly said as she folded her hands and nodded her head. This little Hindu girl in the Amber Fort of Jaipur, India, had jet black hair and wore a bright red dress. Black powder under her eyes made them look even larger than they already were.

Her mother beamed with pride and encouraged her young child to speak to an American traveler with a camera lens where a nose should be.

"Namaste," the little girl again offered.

A voice behind the camera repeated, *"Namaste."*

Namaste.

What a wonderful greeting. It's like saying "Hello," *"Buenos días,"* or *"G'day."* Only sweeter.

It translates: "The God in me honors the God in you."

Namaste.

Namaste

Taj Mahal

India, 1995 · Peace of India

"One rupee."

"Sweets for my baby."

"Buy a necklace."

I shake my head "No." Too many gypsy women. Too many begging children. I have grown cold. My coin pocket holds only lint. These people must whisper to each other, "Americans have money. Let's ravish them." They see me and come running across the desert, leaving only light footprints in the sand. I shield my face to ignore their advances.

It wasn't like that my first week in India. My pockets sang with rupees and gum, combs and pens. But I wasn't prepared for the army of children and women, even holy men, doing their jobs — begging on the streets, in the desert, and in cracks between hotels. The joy of giving soon faded into disappointment and annoyance.

"Please leave me alone."

"I don't have anything for you."

"I've given it all away."

"NO! GO AWAY!"

But this woman, a gypsy in the ghats of Jaisalmer, this woman was gentle. I came to photograph the sunset, the glorious orange ball as it slid behind the domed ghats and disappeared beyond the ancient stone fort. This gypsy woman came quietly and stood at my side. She waited while I adjusted my tripod and checked the lighting. She didn't interrupt with a voice, a worn open palm, or a handful of cheap necklaces chiming in the wind. She stood by me, watching and waiting, patiently waiting. Curious about me, a woman alone, wearing khaki trousers, a photo vest bulging with film, lenses, filters, and notebooks. My eye strayed from the camera and our gazes

Gypsy woman who dwelled in a tent

Women bringing butter lamps to the altar during Diwali

Schoolgirls on a field trip to Agra

Gypsies at Pushkar Camel Fair

"You don't run down the present, pursue it with baited hooks and nets. You wait for it, empty-handed, and you are filled. You have fish left over."

— Annie Dillard

met. She was stunning in her yellow sari, bangles, and bracelets. The *bindi* on her forehead glowed against her dark, smooth skin.

I smiled at her. She slowly smiled back. Her strong eyes locked into mine. "One rupee for my baby," she said, remembering her nomadic duty to beg for a living.

"Do you speak much English?" I asked.

"A little." She seemed surprised that I would actually talk with her.

"How old are you?"

"Twenty-four," was her reply. She had three children with her. The baby was sick. His nose was like a faucet of thick porridge. His chest rattled with every breath.

She asked about my children and was saddened when I said I had three girls. "No boy children?" she kept asking, shaking her head.

"No. Three beautiful daughters and three beautiful granddaughters."

I tried to justify my failure to produce a son. We talked for half an hour, the time it took to photograph her as the light of the sun slipped away.

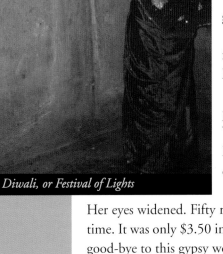
Diwali, or Festival of Lights

We were not Indian and American, gypsy and photographer, beauty and the beast, silk and khaki. We were women. Women talking about our children and our lives. She didn't have an address. She lived in a tent and traveled through the desert. A free life. A hard life.

In parting, I gave her my comb, my pen, and 50 rupees. Her eyes widened. Fifty rupees was a lot to her. She was used to getting one rupee at a time. It was only $3.50 in American currency. I said thank you and good-bye to this gypsy woman and wished her luck in her life.

She caught my arm with her multi-ringed hand, reached down, took off one of her own ankle bracelets and handed it to me.

"A gift," she said softly with a warm glow in her eyes.

"For you, my friend."

India, 1995 · Tears at Raj Ghat

The eternal flame
burned.
A flicker of light
danced,
calling out prayers,
pleas for peace.

I watched a barefoot woman
as she crumbled golden marigolds on the shiny black altar.
She bowed with her eyes fixed on the eternal fire and
a tear slipped down her cheek.
She looked to see if anyone noticed.

Woman placing marigolds on Gandhi's eternal flame altar

Raj Ghat on the Yamuna River in New Delhi
is the cremation site of Mahatma Gandhi.
Mahatma means "great soul."

Gandhi Ji's ashes were scattered in the seas
and all the principal rivers in India.
He is in harmony with nature — in death as he was in life.

People travel far and wide to visit Raj Ghat.
They lay golden marigolds, the holy color,
on the black marble altar.
They kneel in respect for the man who embraced
all life and the grand law of love.

I, too, knelt in that space.
I felt the cold stone on my legs,
inhaled the fragrance of fresh flowers
and stared into the glow of the eternal flame.

Suddenly emotions called out from somewhere deep
within my soul and tears flowed freely.

Tears for Gandhi Ji, a remarkable man
who earned respect from nations.

I cried for all people, for world peace, and compassion for all beings.
Love. Peace. Life.
I wept uncontrollably and unashamed.

Gandhi died the year I was born.
He was gone when I arrived.
Yet,
I knew him.

A mantra is a word or
words chanted as a prayer.

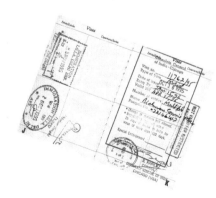

Archway at the Ghats in Jaisalmer

"I hoped that the trip would be the best of all journeys: a journey into ourselves."

— Shirley MacLaine

Little girl on a balcony

India, 1995 · Women's Work

Dung.
Camel dung.
Cow dung.
Horse dung.
The Pushkar Camel Fair welcomes animals and people from all over Rajasthan. India is famous for this *mela*. While men bargain, women and children work. Their duties include collecting dung. Shit. With large baskets and bowls balanced on their heads, they walk barefoot through the desert sands, gracefully squat down to scoop up a pile of dung with their bare hands, and add it to their baskets. Good posture is important.

Woman sorting through basket of dung

When the baskets are full, the collection complete, women return to their camp-sites, roll the dung into small round balls, and spread it out to dry. Dung is used for campfires to warm the family through the cold, to cook meals, and to provide light against the darkness.

I walked by and a woman reached out to shake my hand in an act of friendship and peace. She patted me on the back as we spoke in our own tongues. She continued on her way, filling her basket as she walked with a straight back. Her mark was left.

Dung. Shit on my shoulder, in my hand.

Peace on earth.

Rolling camel dung into balls for campfires

Woman collecting dung

"To understand oneself
is to have compassion
for everything."

— Nagi Gompa Lama

An author ("Battle Hymn of the Republic" poem), reformer, and women's rights activist, Mrs. Howe wrote this Mother's Day Proclamation in 1878:

Cow nursing her calf next to a tank

"Ye are the fruits of one tree and the leaves of one branch...the earth is but one country and mankind its citizens."

— Baha' u' lla'h, 1817–92

Arise then, women of this day!
Arise all women who have hearts,
whether your baptism be that of water or tears!
Say firmly: "We will not have great
questions decided by irrelevant agencies.
Our husbands shall not come to us,
reeking with carnage, for caresses and applause.
Our sons shall not be taken from us to unlearn all that we have
been able to teach them of charity, mercy, and patience.
We women of one country will be too tender of those from another country
to allow our sons to injure theirs.
From the bosom of the devastated earth, a voice goes up with our own.
It says, 'DISARM! DISARM!'"

"...to be a free nation in our own land," Etta sang in a sweet voice, her rifle slung over her shoulder.

Shalom.

A schoolgirl reaching for holy water at a station of the cross in Jerusalem

"Ye are all parts
of one another."

— Muhammad,
The Koran 3:195

A little girl holding a prayer book

Walking through the streets of Jerusalem

"Here I am, safely returned over those peaks from a journey far more beautiful and strange than anything I had hoped for or imagined. How is it that this safe return brings such regret?"

— Peter Matthiessen

Russia, 1990 · Peace Is a Verb

I watched clouds of my own breath freeze into crystals and float into the crisp winter air as I walked through the streets of a small village in the Russian countryside. Ornately carved window frames and doors proudly displayed a near-forgotten craft and seemed out of place amidst paintless, weather-worn houses. As cold as it was, I thought it curious that no smoke curled into the brisk air from chimney stacks.

Time seemed to have abandoned this old village centuries ago. I expected to mingle with village people and get a taste of "real" Russian countryfolk. But there seemed to be none. Why was no one chopping wood to make hearth fires burn? Where were the children? Shouldn't they be out making snowmen, playing in this rare winter sun?

The Kremlin at night

Russian space center, where all space flights are controlled

There are few lights here. Headlights on cars are even very dim.

The toilet paper is very rough (paid five kopecks for toilet paper in bathrooms).

Four of us photographers were standing together talking and we suddenly realized that people thought we were a line and were lining up behind us.

You can trade cigarettes here for almost anything.

I listened closely. No dogs barked. No birds sang. There was no laughter from children. Silence. I heard only the sound of freshly fallen snow crunching under my own boots and the clicking of my camera as I recorded images on film. The village must be abandoned, I thought.

Suddenly, a door creaked open and an old woman emerged, slowly walking toward the wood-slat fence. She watched me closely with no emotion on her face. I smiled and called out, "Hello! Do you speak English?"

She looked at me curiously for a long time. Then she glanced up and down the barren street, perhaps looking for a car or bus, wondering where in the world I came from and why I was here in this tundra alone. "I'm American, visiting Russia to photograph," I offered as a weak explanation.

Silence.

I continued to smile at her. Then slowly the curves of her mouth graduated into a

▼▼

Beautiful gold teeth

Wedding celebration in Moscow

An old Russian tradition was to meet guests with bread and salt.

"Hospitality is a form of worship."
— The Talmud

glorious smile filled with crooked, gold teeth. She waved her hand at me and a constant flow of Russian dialect burst from her lips. She must have had a hundred questions — as did I. We hungrily exchanged words that neither of us understood, yet it satisfied our own curiosity just to communicate. "Where are the children?" I asked. "How many people live in this village? How do you survive out here?"

I felt a warm feeling toward this weathered old woman. She covered my hands with hers as she spoke. I wanted so much to understand the words behind her tenderness.

I commented on her pretty blue scarf. Noticing that it was the same color blue as my gloves, I took them off and gave them to her, pointing to the matching set. She looked at the gloves, turned them over, studying them, and nodded her head in agreement. "Yes, they match all right," is what I think she must have said, and then she handed them back to me.

I said, "No, they are a gift for you," and motioned for her to keep them. She was reluctant. In exchange I raised my camera and asked for a photo. She shyly covered her mouth to hide her teeth — those wonderful, crooked, golden teeth.

Russian woman in the countryside

I bought a watercolor from a famous local artist at "The House of the Artists" commune in Yarslav, where 200 artists live and work in an apartment building built by the state. The artist had to sign a slip for me to take the art out of the country. I paid 150 rubles ($27.27) for a village scene watercolor, and 70 rubles ($12.73) for a chalk drawing of an Estonian fisherman. Beautiful work.

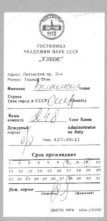

Woman protesting outside the Kremlin

Then she reached out and hugged me from over the fence. It was a big, sincere, strong bear hug. We waved good-bye — both still speaking in languages that were unintelligible to each other. Yet, we both knew and understood the precious exchange of humanity that had just taken place between an American and a Soviet woman.

An exchange of souls that needed no voice.

Beautiful Russian child

Our Russian translator, Lena

Counting with an abacus

Three generations of Russian women

Russian pins

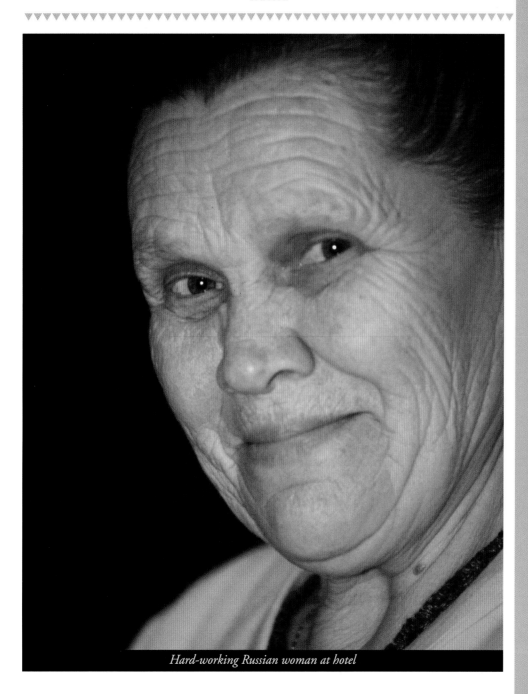

Hard-working Russian woman at hotel

Men and men and women
and women
walk arm in arm or
holding hands.

▼▼▼

Ecuador, 1995 · The Saint of Tonampade

"WELCOME TO TONAMPADE," a sign on the wall greeted missionary guests. It further read: "Except for cleaning out many years of accumulated 'stuff,' as Aunt Rachel finally called it, I have tried to leave this special house as much as possible the way Nimu had it. Kome knows where everything is, pretty much, so feel free to ask him. I have asked him to keep the house for me and he takes the responsibility very seriously. I appreciate any courtesy you show him in this regard."

I sat at a round, wobbly table in the center of crudely hewn floorboards in Rachel's house. Knotted hammocks hung on the wall alongside a large blowgun, parrot feathers, a spear, a feather fan, and a *chimbira* palm dreamcatcher. A feathered headdress and bone breastplate hung next to photos of North American Indians. Twenty-six translations of the New Testament were wrapped in a plastic bag, stacked upon books on a cupboard shelf. A photo of Rachel standing next to Dayuma, her housemate for many

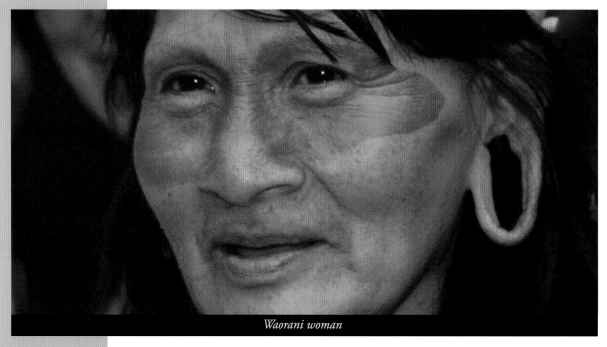

Waorani woman

Waorani woman and child

Woman in mountains

Woman in graveyard

years, hung on the wall. She looked like everyone's smiling, gray-haired grandmother.

Rachel Saint died November 11, 1994, a few months prior to my visit to the jungle village of Tonampade, which translates as "stream of the bat." Rachel's body rests in a small fenced area a few feet from her house. I felt her presence everywhere.

In 1956, a group of missionaries including Nate Saint, Rachel's brother, landed their small aircraft in Waorani (Auca) territory. They landed on a short river beach they named Palm Beach, measuring the length of their "runway" by dropping bags of colored dust at split-second intervals and counting the splashes.

They called their mission "Operation Auca" and from September to January they flew over, lowering baskets of gifts, machetes, kettles, bright shirts, trinkets, and trousers. On the first landing, January 2, they brought a radio, walkie-talkies, tools, food, boards, and sheets of aluminum to build a shelter. They made a camp and shouted Auca phrases into the jungle, "I like you." Then they prayed.

On January 6, the missionaries came face-to-face with naked natives, a man and two women. They recorded it as a "friendly" encounter and Nate took the man for a plane ride over the beach and village. "He shouted with joy all the way there and back," Nate wrote in his diary. What Nate interpreted as joy may have turned out to be fear. The natives didn't return the next day.

Dayuma

Nate flew to home base at Shell Mera to see his sister, Rachel, and his wife, Mary, and he gave them film he had taken of the Auca natives. Sunday, January 8, Nate took a short flight over the makeshift missionary village and noted in his diary that none of his men were in sight. He called on his plane radio. No answer. He called home base and reported that he would call again at 4:35.

At 4:35 there was silence. The following day a plane was sent to investigate. They reported the missionary plane demolished and Nate's body floating in the river. Ecuadorian soldiers, guides, and other missionaries started into the jungle on foot. U.S. Air Force Rescue Services sent planes from Panama. Pilot Major Malcolm Numberg located four more bodies downstream. One body was never found, only a pair of sneakers.

A common grave was dug and the men were buried in simple ceremony under a tropical rain.

The Saint family was well known for their work throughout the world. *Life Magazine* and *Reader's Digest* featured the story along with worldwide reports in newspapers and television. "Missionaries Killed by Auca Natives in the Jungles of Ecuador."

Sitting in Rachel's house I read portions of Nate's diary and realized that the media had missed the most incredible part of the story.

After Nate's death, Rachel took it upon herself to befriend the natives that killed her brother. After much patience and bravery, she not only succeeded in spreading the "word of God," but ended up living in the village for the rest of her life. The natives built her a house complete with a "modern" bathroom. This house became home to many missionaries for the next forty years. Rachel was a teacher, nurse, spiritual mentor, and a friend to the natives. As a young girl, Dayuma, who later became her best friend, had reportedly been part of the warring party that killed Nate Saint.

I spoke with Dayuma about the killings. She said that Mincaye, one of the elders who voted to kill the missionaries, still lived in the village but he was very old and I couldn't speak with him.

But she remembered. Her Uncle Nampa was one of the elders that said the men were evil with their big flying bird and shiny trinkets.

"He really started the war party but Gekita was blamed for it," she admitted. "It wasn't at all like what the news reports said. The missionaries got frightened first and shot Nampa. We had never seen guns before and it made things worse. We dragged Nampa into the jungle and went back and killed the men with our *chonta* spears. The elders believed it was the only way we could protect our people from men who brought evil into our village. At that time we were used to fighting and killing natives from other tribes. It wasn't much different."

Missionary story versus native story, equally interesting, each speaking their own truth.

The candle's light flickered on a rusty oil barrel under the screen window next to my bed. Rachel's bed. Dayuma and her family noisily visited in her wooden hut across the darkness. A baby cried, children laughed, life continued.

Thoughts of Rachel were heavy in my mind as I lay curled up on her mattress under camouflaged mosquito netting. She left her mark, spiritually. She also left a legacy of love and goodwill. The people in this village fondly called her "Star."

Rachel's mission will never end. Her work continues through the people who live here, people like Dayuma, who greet visitors with a smile and a handshake and a shared pot of *chicha*.

God has touched this place.

I bought two rag dolls in Quito, handmade from old fabric, for 17,000 sucres ($5.00 U.S.). Paid 2,000 sucres ($.60 U.S.) to swim in the hot springs in Banos. Spent 3,000 sucres ($1.20 U.S.) to see the movie *Casablanca*. We sat on folding chairs in a room and watched it on a TV with a VCR! Popcorn was $.10 U.S.

Hacienda woman and child

Wash day in Dubrovnik

Yugoslavia, 1990 · Village of Miracles

There seems to be a similarity in the travel of clouds to meet the sun and the travel of humans to Medugorje.

Medugorje is a Herzegovinian village unmarked on the maps of Europe. A region among mountains rich only in rock, it was virtually unknown to the world until Mary decided to move in. That was enough for millions to make the pilgrimage from all directions and all corners of the world. Every day. Thanks to Mother Mary, the unknown became known and the distant became near.

The church in Medugorje, seen through the vineyard

I met a new friend, Susan, in Medugorje and we exchanged Christmas gifts. I gave her a clean pair of my wool socks (our rooms had no heat and she was always cold) and she gave me a piece of bramble bush from the area where the children first saw the Virgin Mary. Treasures — the gifts, and Susan.

Susan invited me to Rome to visit for a couple of weeks. I'm going back to Dubrovnik for a few days and then will take her up on her offer.

A rosary that had turned into gold

Part of the miracle is seeing crowds of every race, nation, and opposing view sitting on wooden benches in the Church of St. Jacob or kneeling beneath the white stone cross on the hill of Krizevac. The simple and the theologian, the uneducated and the philosopher, Croatians, Slavs, Germans, Italians, Americans, people of all languages, side by side in song, prayer, and deep meditation. Perfumed women in lavish fur coats sit next to Croatian grandmothers wearing layers of tattered clothing, long black leggings, and hand-knit scarves.

These people pour out their dreams, yearnings, and fears. They glance toward the white Virgin statue in the front of the church. Eyes meet eyes and it is as if everything has been said and heard. Their prayers are all received with the same grace, with the same love.

This gathering is the most original, open, and sincere conference of nations uniting in a prayer for peace. It happens every day in Medugorje under the guidance of the Virgin Mary. Yugoslavian and foreign visitors alike come to meet the Virgin and hear the story of the six children who witnessed her apparition in June of 1982 when the Madonna, Queen of Peace, appeared to them. Pilgrims come to hear, see, and touch the remaining visionary children, Ivan, Vicka, and Marija, now adults, who reside in Medugorje and continue to receive Mary's messages.

At first Mary appeared to the visionaries daily, praying and giving messages, answering their questions. From March 1, 1984, until the beginning of 1987 she gave weekly messages to the parish of Medugorje and people throughout the world. On January 25, 1987, monthly messages began on the 25th of each month. The messages continue.

I, too, traveled to this Yugoslavian village and walked the path through vineyards where the apparitions appeared to Crnica Hill. I traveled to the Bijakovici village of Podbrdo, up a worn, rocky path to where the Virgin first appeared. Sheep and goats wandered freely through the

There are three main religions here: Roman Catholic, Orthodox, and Islam.

Statue of Mother Mary in church square, with rosary

mountainside among crude wood crosses and thorn bushes. Old women robed in black and young girls in jeans and sweatshirts prayed the rosary during the forty-five-minute climb up the steep side of the mountain. People tucked letters, prayers, and photos of their loved ones between the sharp crevices of rocks.

The old and weary climbed this steep rocky hill. Men and women with crutches and canes climbed with conviction, receiving helping hands from strangers. Some carried their shoes, as bloodied feet were a wanted sacrifice. Others traveled great distances on their knees. At one point an elderly Croatian woman dropped to the ground, pointed toward the heavens and called out, "The sun is spinning!"

I looked and saw the sun appear to be changing colors. It was white with a black center, with pinks and blues spinning around it. The colors converged and grew into a deep, blood red. All around rays were emanating into a large sphere, a spectacular sign.

I climbed and prayed for my family and friends. I asked for peace and love in my heart and understanding and knowledge in my being. I rested serenely among the rocks above the village. A cool wind gently blew. The radiant sun warmed my face. Common sounds of barking dogs and workers in the village below intertwined with the hum of praying pilgrims and the falling of small

Croatian woman knitting as she tends sheep

Dubrovnik is on the Dalmatian coast. The old city is a walled fort, with a moat around the entire city. There are two drawbridges you cross to enter. No motorized vehicles are allowed. For $1.00 (U.S.) you can climb up the stairs to the top of the wall, and walk around the entire city, which juts out into the sea. Every day I was in Dubrovnik, I walked the wall. In one direction I could look out to the sea, in another I could look up into the mountains that protect the village, or I could look down into the busy everyday life of the people in the city. It was breathtaking and humbling.

rocks loosened by climbers' feet. A breathtaking view of snowcapped mountains surrounded me. I sat and wondered if we really need to travel to a place of tranquillity, no matter where in the world it is, to find our inner peace?

I understand why people are touched by their journey to Medugorje. It gives them time for peace and thought and inspiration for a pure life of giving, healing, and helping others. It is easy to spread a loving message of peace when you experience it first in your own heart. People come here desperate and leave happy. They come tired and leave rested. They come poor and leave rich in faith and belief. The spiritual cure is obvious and, often, so is the physical.

I crowded around the cross with the others as Ivan and Vicka lead a prayer group. The sun was beginning to disappear behind the mountain and somewhere in the background a guitar strummed a soft tune. It was Christmas Eve.

After a period of silent prayer, Vicka announced that the Virgin Mary was here to

Yugoslavia uses two alphabets (Cyrillic in the south and east and the Latin alphabet in the north and west), and has three main languages: Serbo-Croatian, Slovenian, and Macedonian.

Woman praying on Crnica Hill

Cross on Krizevac Hill

"Help thy sister's boat across, and Lo! thine own has reached the shore."

— Hindu proverb

give us a message. "The Madonna said, 'I am joyously happy all of you are here.' The Madonna spread her hands over the entire crowd and gave her blessing to each person individually. She said, 'My children, go in peace.' She was accompanied by three angels."

Ivan added, "Our Lady came in great glory. She brought three angels with her. I can find no words to express her joy. She held her arms out over us and blessed each one of us. She said to present all our problems to her and to be very joyful. She prayed one Our Father and Glory Be. She said, 'Go in God's peace, my dear children,' and she left amidst bright lights, making a cross of light as she went back up into the heavens."

Ivan and Vicka lit candles and people began to sing in their own tongues. Simultaneously, words of song and praise were offered up in Italian, German, Croatian, French, Spanish, and English. Women began to weep in joyful emotion. A string of candlelight filed down the hill, winding its way to the bottom. The sky was clear and filled with stars. It seemed like some had floated to earth to join in the vigil and light our path.

That night I went to midnight mass at St. Jacob. The church was so crowded that I stood outside for part of the mass. Then, somehow, I was lucky enough to be able to find a standing spot in the balcony where I could take in the beauty of the church and the ceremony below. Father Slavco spoke, repeating his messages in six languages. Members of the crowd appeared with their musical instruments and joined in the orchestra. A blind woman came forward and sang beautiful songs she had written herself. Inspiration was at a peak. People didn't begin to leave until after 2:00 A.M. when Father Slavco finally said we had to go home!

I climbed Krizevac, Hill of the Cross, on Christmas Day. This hill was steeper than the one at Podbrdo. As I walked the two miles and wandered through the vineyards to make my way to the foot of the mountain, I encountered many shepherd women tending their flocks. I stopped and "talked" with an elderly Croatian woman who was knitting a sweater while watching her sheep. She smiled and spoke politely to me, nodded toward Krizevac with approval and understanding, and pointed me on to the correct pathway. The grassy trail wound into stone and I lost my direction. Another woman chopping wood by a stone building stopped and pointed the way for me to go. She stood watching to be sure I made the right turns. A second time I lost myself in thought and another woman offered the way. Angels were guiding me.

Arriving at the first station of the cross I began the uphill climb. A German shepherd dog came to sniff my shoes. She looked up at me, wagged her tail, and turned up the path. She stopped and looked at me, waiting for me to follow. Another guide. Each time I stopped to catch my breath or take a photo, or to pray at a station of the cross, this dog sat and waited for me. Where there were two paths she waited until I caught up to follow her in the right direction. When I stopped to write she curled up at my feet and patiently waited for me to finish, sitting with me for an hour.

After an hour of prayer, observation, and writing, I began my climb down. My pal, the German shepherd, guided me halfway down and then must have decided I would

I went to the market and bought a fresh loaf of bread (less than 30 cents) and a hunk of cheese or fruit every day. It was at the end of my trip and all I could afford. I had packets of hot chocolate and soup broth in my room. I stayed at a house for $15 a day, renting someone's bedroom; no heat, but the owner brought me hot water and tea every morning and evening.

Father Jozo with a painting of Mary on the wall

Praying among the crosses

be okay because she barked at me three times, then turned to greet another woman on her uphill journey. What a loving home this dog has and what a meaningful job. A guide for pilgrims!

I had journeyed to Medugorje with a vision — a photojournalistic vision of an inspirational story in this small village of miracles. A vision of photographing old women wearing ragged coats, their gnarled, wrinkled hands grasping worn rosaries as they knelt before the cross. And, perhaps, images of a small child curiously, yet gently, reaching out to kiss the cheek of the white Madonna statue. I came with a vision of wonderful photographs clicking through my mind, but I left with much more.

I left with a vision of peace and hope for all mankind.

In a special prayer session, Father Jozo Zokov said, "As you leave Medugorje carry light and peace within your hearts back into the world. If only we could see how quickly the world would change and peace would be restored when we live in love."

Live in love. Pray for peace.

Walking in the rain in Belgrade

Oldest African woman in Trinidad

Trinidad, 1995 · Celebration of Peace

Driving by a Hindu temple in Trinidad, we noticed a sign announcing "125th anniversary." We stopped the car and I stuck my camera out the window to photograph the colorfully dressed women walking into the temple. Two men in suits saw me and came over to the car. Two of my daughters, Kelli and Nicole, were with me. They looked at me with an, "Oh, oh, now you've done it," expression.

The men leaned into the window and asked where we were from. I said, "The States."

He said, "Oh, so you are an American photographer."

"Yes," I replied.

"Well, then come in. We welcome you."

The temple was very ornate inside. Incense burned, the altar was decorated with flowers, and delicious food was arranged on tables. Music played. A Hindu priest sat yoga-style with his hands in a Buddha position, silently praying.

Two women were being honored during this celebration: the oldest African woman (ninety-five) and the oldest Indian (seventy-three) woman in the community. This was the first time they had met. As elders they hold a place of honor. For them to meet, exchange flowers, words, and participate in a special ceremony, was a symbol for others to honor all cultures and religions and strive for world peace. A simple ceremony. A strong message.

The oldest women in the community

Oldest Indian woman with her granddaughter

Tobago, 1995 · Mama Dlo (Mother of the Water)

Today I am sitting on the beach on the island of Tobago an island in the West Indies. The sun is glorious and the wind blows gently on my face. During my travels the past few days I have picked up a book of island folklore and legends. The islands are steeped in legend and I find them fascinating. I have been reading about an island

Mama Dlo?

goddess named Mama Dlo or Mama Dglo. The name is derived from the French word meaning "mother of the water." The lower half of her body takes the form of a *houilla,* or anaconda, snake. Sometimes her upper half is a hideous old woman. She is said to be the lover of Papa Bois, the legendary "old man of the high woods." Mortal men who commit crimes against the forest, such as burning down trees or indiscriminately putting animals to death or fouling the rivers, could find themselves "married" to her for life. To protect themselves from Mama Dlo in the forest, men take off their left shoes, turn them upside down, and immediately walk away, backwards, until they reach home.

Other times Mama Dlo takes the form of a beautiful woman singing silent songs on still afternoons, sitting at the water's edge in the sunlight.

I sit with the folklore book open on my lap, my camera nearby. The beach is filled with sunbathers, swimmers, and children playing. Looking up, I see the form of a woman, alone, with no one else around her. It is unusual that the small section of the beach this woman is sitting on is so empty. I reach for my camera and focus on her. Her form is beautiful, no features, just a black silhouette against the water. It looks as if she has no legs, with just a body resting upon the beach, her hands reaching out to filter handfuls of sand through her fingers. The tide rushes in around her and flows back to the sea.

My attention returns to the book, "Mama Dlo lingers for a golden moment, and in a flash of green, she is gone. 'Did you see a fish jump?' 'Yes, but it did not go back again!' Nothing but a big Morte Bleu, rising in the sun beams."

I look up and she is gone. It has been only seconds.

Mama Dlo? Island folklore? Goosebumps crawl across my skin. I think I should return to the mountains.

United States, 1986 · Death or Birth?

I stood weeping before my mother. Tears flooded my eyes, rolling down my cheeks, staining my face. I couldn't . . . didn't want to hold back my grief. I wanted her. I needed her. I missed her.

I wanted to share how I felt with her. I needed the reassurance only a mother can give. I wanted her to talk to me, to hold me and tell me that it's okay to feel, to love . . . to cry. I didn't know if I was crying for myself — for my loneliness, my loss, my emptiness — or for her. Why did she leave me?

Suddenly I felt a gentle wave of peace, like a reassuring hand softly resting upon my shoulder. A familiar voice, yet unspoken, engulfed my thoughts. The message was clear: "Why do you weep? This body lying before you is only a form, a means of existence while on this earth. An expression for the soul. Your mother, my being, my essence, is not gone from you. I will always be with you as I have in many past times and as I will be again. I will always love you."

At that instant I knew. She is here. She is beside me, within me, surrounding me, and always guiding me. Her spirit will speak to me in my thoughts. In my dreams we will live and laugh and play as we always have. I can visualize her standing near me in physical form, yet I know she is just indulging me, as a mother would a child, so I can easily perceive her in the form I knew.

I will always feel a wave of sadness when I think of my mother, because I do miss her. Yet, I quietly feel an awakening. A rejoicing! What peace she has! My mother has not died. She has only shed an earthly form that caused her much physical pain. She is still here, with joy and happiness. She has found balance and love. She has found God.

My mother is everywhere. Her kind face shines in the soft petals of a flower. Her loving smile dances on the reflection of a sunlit stream. Her friendly laughter sings on the gentle breeze. The radiant light of her inner being will warm my heart forever. She knows the depth of my love.

And I know.

This is not death. My mother has passed from this earthly womb and now she is free. She is Light.

She has just been born.

My mother, 1948

Chile, 2000 · Shantytown Women

Perhaps no other trip I have taken has affected me as much as my travels to document the shantytown women of Chile. My heart split wide open as I experienced true everyday compassion expressed through sharing with others when you have only two eggs in your cupboard. When you have no medicine, no money, no family.

Most of the women I met lived in houses made from bits and pieces of wood, tin, cardboard — whatever they could salvage. But they "owned" their own houses and the small square of land they sat upon. They were not homeless. One woman offered me a bowl of corn when I visited. I tried to tell her I wasn't hungry but she insisted, with a contented smile on her face. I ate slowly and reluctantly.

I traveled to Santiago and Concepción to photograph shantytown women for a project headed by an Owatonna, Minnesota, woman. Karen Anderson was one of the founders of Educación Popular en Salud (EPES), a community-based health project of

One-room stilt home on the river's backwater

"One's little world is put into perspective by the bigger world out there."

— Gain Rubin Bereny

the Evangelical Lutheran Church in Chile. EPES works to improve the health and well-being of shantytown communities through the organized participation of the people themselves. EPES health teams educate shantytown women, allowing them to study and graduate into becoming health promoters in their own neighborhoods.

These women learn to give shots and medication and to diagnose the signs and symptoms of acute respiratory infections and determine when a child with pneumonia needs to go to the clinic. When women discover they can gain a little control over one of the main causes of death in children, they also find they can change other things that affect their community's health and, ultimately, their own lives.

Rosa, a grandmother and one of the early health promoters, revealed, "When I first entered the group, I felt useless, that I was wasting my life. I felt insecure. I just let things happen, accepted them passively. This depressed me and was driving me mad. Entering the group permitted me to make decisions. To participate has rejuvenated me. I have recovered myself, my sleeping dreams."

Women who before would not even go outside because they had no self-esteem are now relentlessly banging on the doors of government and health officials to force them to offer better programs for AIDS, rape, and domestic violence victims. They are saving their own lives through saving the lives of others.

Dumas, *healthcare providers who heal with herbs and plants*

"I learned to face problems and to say what I want, and also to ask questions. Now, I know I can defend myself, open my mouth, learn that I am able," reported another shantytown woman.

I met Valeria, a health promoter who has worked her way through college and is now a great inspiration to others; Soledad, the first shantytown woman to head the Lutheran women's organization throughout the Southern Cone of Latin America; Monica, who has saved many lives in her community and whose health team's ground-breaking work on women, poverty, and AIDS won her a full scholarship to the world AIDS congress. I met Rosa, the health promoter who wrote a book about shantytown women and the terror they lived during the assassination of President Salvador Allende and the loss of loved ones during the following military coup of General Pinochet's dictatorship.

The compassion and guidance of these and other men and women of EPES have inspired others to take charge of their lives. Communities plagued by millions of rats organized to clean up garbage areas. City officials were forced to provide water and sewage systems. Women formed small worker-run collectives to produce local crafts to sell. Others have organized cooperative day care and support groups for abused women and children.

Graduating to become shantytown health providers

Preparing for graduation

One woman said, "We, the marginalized, the slum dwellers, the professionals, the prostitutes, the homosexuals, the youth and children, all need to join together to change this country."

These women are responsible for bringing neighbors and communities together to confront their difficulties and to improve their lives through cooperation.

I was equally inspired by Karen, who has been working to unite the efforts of the women of Chile through the intense urging of her own compassionate heart. She said, "My work is about providing an opportunity for people to develop their gifts and talents. We are all well aware of the injustice in our world. The number of people living in abject poverty is at an all-time high. And yet we know the biggest obstacles to reaching proper health for all are not technical problems, but rather social and political problems. Everyone has the right to be dealt with justly and to stand up for justice."

Three generations of strong women

▼▼▼

I listened to one inspiring story after another as I traveled from house to house in several shantytowns, El Bosque, The Toma, Hualpancillo. I was privileged to attend a graduation ceremony of a group of women as new health promoters. This was the first group to be trained entirely by another group of shantytown women. The women's speeches that night were all about dignity. Even though they are poor and times are bad, they have their dignity, and the men, women, and children present applauded them with pride.

A first anniversary of the land takeover, which created this shantytown, was also being celebrated that evening. Within a year the community had managed to obtain electricity and had gotten the city to provide satellite toilets along the dirt streets. There were more than 12,000 people living in this shantytown.

Experiencing the shantytown women of Santiago and Concepción, sharing corn and exchanging hugs, continues to haunt me. Meeting these incredibly poor yet strong women and listening to their stories of hope and commitment made me look at my own values and all my "stuff." Do I actually need even half of what I own? What is really important in this world? Money? Ego? Material belongings? Social status? Or does it come right back to the basics — love, health, happiness, humor, respect, honesty, and compassion.

One shantytown woman told me, "We are no longer the same. We have made ourselves see."

Knowing each one of us has the ability to make a difference in someone's life, even if it is as simple as a smile, is a big responsibility.

> "A journey is a person in itself; no two are alike. And all plans, safeguards, policies, and coercion are fruitless. We find after years of struggle that we do not take a trip; a trip takes us."
>
> — John Steinbeck

Mother and daughters in Concepción

Afterword

It is my hope to encourage all women to accept each new challenge in their lives with a sense of adventure, a way to learn and gain knowledge of one's own purpose. As we grow spiritually back toward our source we discover life is an endless chain of adventure.

When we change our consciousness, living positively, intuitively, and spiritually, we hear a voice within ourselves. It may speak faintly at first, but if we listen closely it will grow more distinct. One day it will thunder inside us and we will come home and reconnect with the highest level of our consciousness, Goddess/God/Universe. We will remember to trust our feminine, intuitive gifts, gifts we had at birth.

Though we may travel far and in many directions, we will meet only what we carry with us, for every being is a mirror to our own divine self. If we live with compassion, we will grow compassion; if we live in fear we will gather fear. If we live in love, we will be love.

Journey far...

Walk in peace.

"Women have always yearned for faraway places. It was no accident that a woman financed the first package tour of the New World, and you can bet Isabella would have taken the trip herself, only Ferdinand wouldn't let her go."

— Roslyn Friedman

My traveling boots

About Connie Bickman

Connie Bickman has a passion for travel and is inspired by the cultural diversity of people around the world. This passion has taken her to far corners of the earth, more than thirty underdeveloped countries, in search of adventure and the opportunity to photograph and document native cultures, the environment, and humanitarian issues. She has won regional and international awards for both her photography and writing.

Connie is co-owner, publisher, and editor of an inspirational newspaper called *Turtle River Press.* She is also the author of a series of ten children's textbooks, *Through the Eyes of Children* (Abdo and Daughter, publisher).

"Each and every one of us has talents that are given to us as gifts to be shared," she states. "My soul's purpose is simply to be a messenger. I feel I was given the opportunity to travel and the ability to record what I encountered as adventures unfolded into spiritual awakenings. I know my travels are meant to be shared, in hopes they will inspire others to follow their inner voice, dance to the beat of their own drum, and honor the strength and wisdom of the Goddess within."

Connie lives in Minnesota with her cat, Ghinsu. She is surrounded by her own tribe of women, three "beautiful" daughters and five "exceptionally smart" granddaughters.

New World Library
is dedicated to publishing books and audiocassettes
that inspire and challenge us to improve
the quality of our lives and our world.

Our books and tapes are available
in bookstores everywhere.
For a catalog of our complete library
of fine books and cassettes, contact:

New World Library
14 Pamaron Way
Novato, CA 94949

Phone: (415) 884-2100
Fax: (415) 884-2199
Or call toll-free (800) 972-6657
Catalog requests: Ext. 50
Ordering: Ext. 52

E-mail: escort@nwlib.com
www.newworldlibrary.com